MOM AND DAD, WHY DO I NEED TO KNOW MY ARMENIAN HERITAGE?

WRITT...

T...

KC...

ILLUS...TED BY

SELINEH SHAHBAZIAN

Mom and Dad, Why Do I Need to Know My ARMENIAN Heritage?

written by
TALAR KEOSEYAN KOZIKOUJEKIAN

illustrated by
SELINEH SHAHBAZIAN

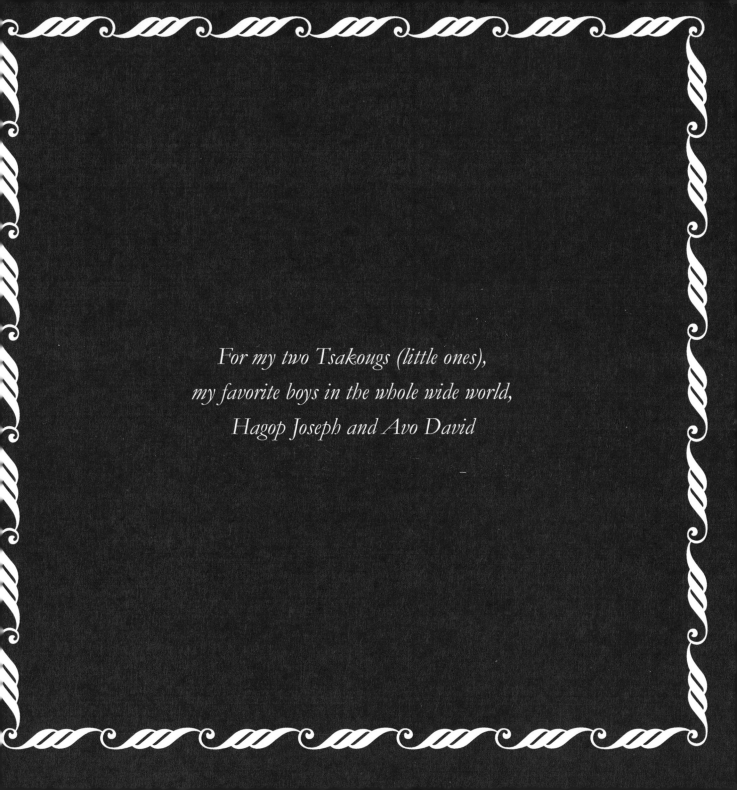

For my two Tsakougs (little ones),
my favorite boys in the whole wide world,
Hagop Joseph and Avo David

"Deghas, (my son), Hagop, get ready to go to bed. Make sure your teeth are brushed and you have said your prayers, especially Der Im Asdvadz."

"I don't understand why I have to say that Armenian prayer. Mom, how many times do I need to remind you that I want to be called Jack, not Hagop? Can we forget all of this Armenian stuff already?"

"Deghas, how can you say that? How can you forget your roots? You have your grandfather's strong Armenian name and you're named after a saint," replied his mom in a sweet and tolerant voice. She was a petite woman, but full of strength. She was raised in America, but valued her heritage. She wanted her children to take pride in being American as well as being Armenian. She wanted Hagop and Avo to embrace both cultures, but was having a difficult time getting the message across, especially to Hagop, who was a spunky little boy in fifth grade. Hagop was a very bright student. He paid attention in all of his classes except Armenian class. He knew the history, but thought he would never need it, so why bother really thinking about it? His Armenian teacher, Mrs. Nazik, knew he had a lot of potential, but was also having a hard time tapping into it. He was a straight A student, except in Armenian class, where he just wanted to be the class clown.

"But Mom, we live in America. I don't want to be different. I don't want people messing up my name. It would just be easier if they called me Jack."

"Get some sleep now. We'll talk about this in the morning on our way to school. Kees-her paree, Tsakoug. I love you." (Good night, little one)

"Good night, Mom."

Jack couldn't understand what the big deal was about. Who cared about being Armenian? Armenia was thousands of miles away. He really couldn't relate. All he heard day in and day out was "speak Armenian, Hagop, keep the culture, Hagop, and value the traditions, Hagop." He didn't care. He wasn't too thrilled about going to church on Sundays or to Armenian school.

Jack pressed the hand of his plush toy that said the "Der Im Asdvadz" prayer and tried to go to sleep. He was tossing and turning. Why this constant bombardment and pressure to be Armenian? He really didn't care. He couldn't wait to get out of Armenian school.

Jack finally fell asleep and began to dream. He saw a beautiful mountain, surrounded by lush green meadows and fields. He saw snow on the mountain caps and was amazed at the beauty and strength of the mountain. Then he saw a fence and was startled. What was going on? Where was he?

An older gentleman was walking by so Jack began to ask him where he was. "Parev, eench bes yes? Toon ches kider vor Hayastan es?" (Hello. How are you? Don't you know that you're in Armenia?)

"Armenia! What am I doing here? I want to go back home to America. How can I get back?"

"Well, Palig Jan (dear child), I think you have been sent here on a mission. Let's walk around and see. Do you see that majestic mountain? That is Mt. Ararat. That is our mountain, but today it stands in Turkey."

"Why is Mt. Ararat in Turkey? Mt. Ararat is Armenian. I don't understand," said Jack.

"I thought you didn't care about Armenia and learning your heritage. Why the change?"

"I don't care. I've heard about Mt. Ararat from Mrs. Nazik. I haven't paid attention though. But now I'm curious. How come Mt. Ararat stands apart from Armenia?"

"That is a long story. Are you sure you want to hear it?"

"Yes, I'm interested. Please tell me."

"Let me introduce myself. My name is Movses Khorenatsi. I am known to everyone as the Father of Armenian History (Badmahayr), because I was the first to write the story of our people. You see Hagop, the reason you are called Hye (Armenian) and the reason your homeland is called Hayastan (Armenia) is because of Haig Nahabed, the founder of our homeland and chief of the most powerful tribes, the Armens. I do believe I have been sent here to remind you about your valiant heritage. Mt. Ararat is where Noah's Ark landed. It is also the symbol of the Armenian nation. Armenia was once a huge country that stretched from the Black to the Caspian to the Mediterranean Seas. It had dynasties, kings, queens, heroes, and heroines. We were the first nation to accept Christianity in 301 A.D. when St. Gregory the Illuminator converted King Dertad III. King Dertad made Christianity the official religion of Armenia. In 451 A.D., Vartan Mamigonian led the country into battle against the fire worshipping Persian army. Although Armenia lost the battle, it won the war and kept its Christian faith."

"Wow, we have been around for a long time! I never realized how much our faith meant to us. Maybe now I can understand why my mom bothers me all the time about going to church and saying my prayers."

"Thank you, Mr. Movses. By the way, my name is Jack. I was wondering if you could tell me more, please?" he asked eagerly.

"Jan (dear), there's so much more history to tell. Armenians are courageous people that have endured many hardships and trials. We have been victims of genocide and ruthless killings. We have had our homes burned, our churches scorched, our language denied. But we have always survived. That is what makes us invincible."

Movses Khorenatsi continued, "The Armenian alphabet was founded by St. Mesrob Mashdots and is comprised of 38 gorgeous and glorious letters. The Armenian culture flourished under the Armenian Dynasties. Later invaders known as Turks came to Armenia and took control. Those were the dark times because we were denied our heritage. We couldn't keep our culture and we prayed in fear. After years of struggling with the Ottoman Empire, an event occurred during World War I that nearly broke the Armenian people."

"Oh no, the Armenian Genocide, right? Every year we take flowers to school and have a Mass for the victims. But I never really realized why we still do this after so many years."

"Yes, the Armenian Genocide. You have to promise to never forget."

"I promise I won't. My Grandmother Araxi and Grandfather Hagop told me the terrible stories of what happened to their parents, but I couldn't really imagine it. Please tell me more about the Armenian Genocide."

"All right. In 1915, the Ottoman Turkish government decided to do away with the Armenians because they wanted only Turks to occupy our lands. They wanted to build a huge empire that had only people who would be of their religion and their culture. In order to accomplish this, they made our ancestors suffer terribly and walk the Syrian desert of Der Zor; more than one and a half million Armenians died. However, our will to survive and thrive was greater. You will see evidence of our great strength and endurance throughout our noble history."

"Mr. Movses Khorenatsi, why did the Ottoman Turkish government kill so many Armenians? They were innocent. I have heard all of this but now with *you* telling me, I understand. It makes me very upset."

"Well, Jack, the very sad part about all of this is that to this day they still do not want to admit to the Armenian Genocide. That is one of the most painful denials."

"What you have told me has really made me think. Now it all makes more sense. I realize why my mom, dad, and Mrs. Nazik, are always trying to help me understand the value of my culture. We have suffered tremendously and do not deserve to be forgotten."

"I don't want to be called Jack anymore!" proclaimed Hagop. "Please call me by my real name: Hagop. Now I understand why my mom and dad are always telling me to speak Armenian, to go to Armenian school, and to study my Bible lessons. I want to know more now. What happened next?"

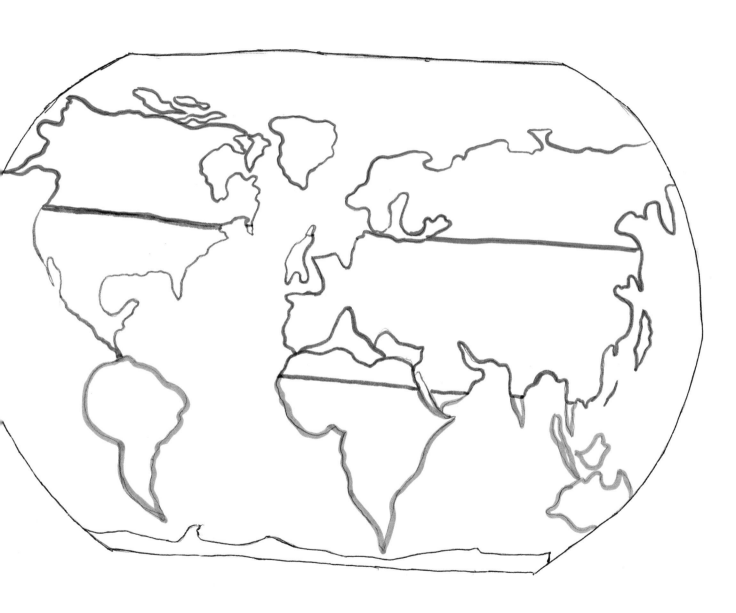

"Well, Hagop, as a result of the Armenian Genocide, we dispersed all around the world. Now there are Armenians practically in every corner of this planet. The first mission of every Armenian dispersed around the world was to construct an Armenian church to help keep our heritage and culture alive. In 1918, Armenia became independent for two years, but due to starvation and enemy threats, decided to join the Soviet Union. Armenia was one of the most literate and highly educated republics. In 1988, Armenians from the Karabagh (Artsakh) region of Azerbaijan joined their brothers and sisters in Armenia to demand freedom and self-rule. Karabagh was Armenian land that was given to Azerbaijan in 1923. Armenians in Karabagh were deprived of their heritage and culture. They revolted in 1988 for justice. After many years in battle, Karabagh became a free and autonomous state. Meanwhile, in Armenia a great catastrophe occurred. On Dec. 7, 1988, a very strong earthquake shook Armenia's second largest city, Leninakan (Gyumri), and again many Armenians lost their lives. We are still recovering from that misfortunate day."

"My mom mentioned to me that she was young at the time of the Armenian earthquake and remembers the whole world coming to the aid of Armenia. She remembers seeing the horrible images on TV. After viewing the sorrow and grief in the peoples' eyes, she wanted to do something to help out. She said that was a turning point in her life. She had to help her fellow Armenians. After discussing her feelings with her cousins, they decided to go to the local market and ask if they could collect donations. The market owner was so touched that the youth wanted to help people so far away that he gladly agreed."

"Yes, the world did come to Armenia's aid. Many people died, yet the will to survive was still strong. Right around this time, Armenians began to demand self rule and wanted their independence from the Soviet Union. On September 21, 1991, Armenia declared its independence and became a free Republic."

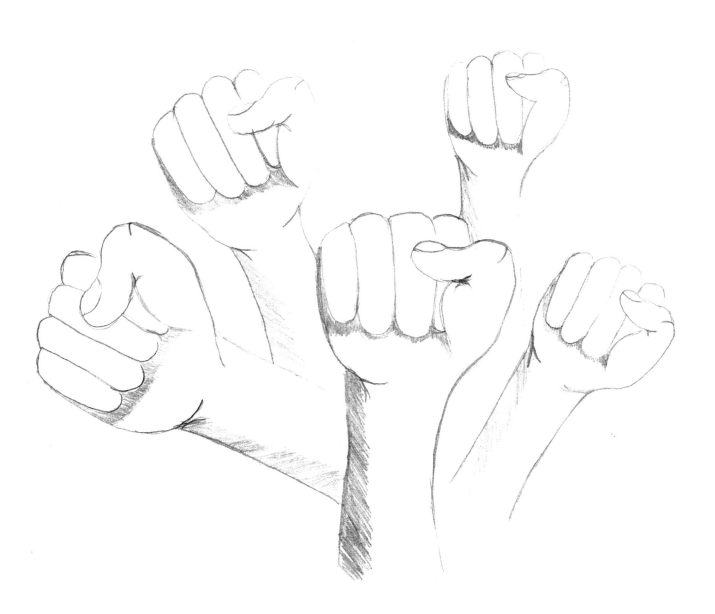

"Baron (Mr.) Khorenatsi, now I understand why my mom and dad sacrifice many things to put Avo and me through Armenian school. *Now* I know why they are so concerned about remaining Armenian. They want to preserve our heritage. I *now* realize why Mrs. Nazik is always trying to get my attention in class and always encouraging me to dig deeper. I'm the one that never pays attention. I have heard all of these stories before but now that I have *seen my* culture and homeland, I know where Armenia is…it is in my heart. I have to do my best to teach all of my friends, Armenians and non-Armenians, about my history and culture. I am Hagop and a proud Armenian-American. I will always be respectful of my roots and religion. Thank you for reminding me how important it is to be Armenian. Tsedesootiun (good-bye)."

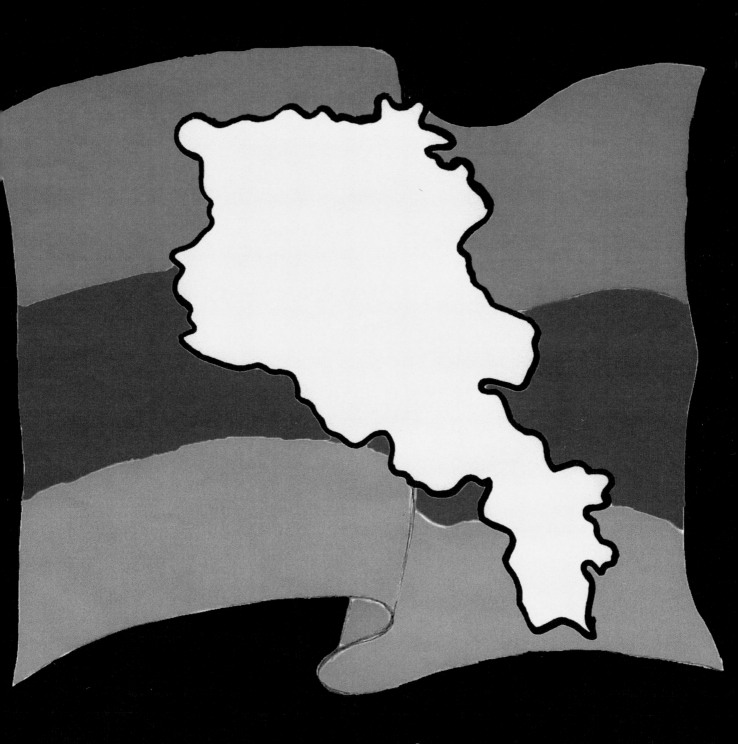

Hagop was startled from his sleep by the sound of the alarm clock.

"Paree looys, Hagop, sorry, I mean *Jack*," greeted his mom.

"Paree looys, Mama. Im anoones Hagop eh." (My name is Hagop)

"Wow, you finally want to be called Hagop? What a wonderful surprise!"

"Mom, I never realized how strong our people are. I now understand what you, dad, and Mrs. Nazik mean when you tell us to be proud of our roots. Baron Movses Khorenatsi explained everything to me."

"How did you speak to Movses Khorenatsi, Hagop Jan?"

"Mom, I saw him in my dream and he led me through Armenian history. I now understand what a strong and rich history Armenia has. I have to go wake up Avo and tell him right now. I'm also going to tell him to stop calling himself Abe. Mom, what time is Armenian school? I can't wait."

"OK, Hagop, I would like to know what else Baron Moves Khorenatsi told you. You must tell me the whole story. Let's get ready for Armenian school now! We have to leave by 7:45 a.m. to make it to school by 8 o'clock. I have never seen you so excited. You're making my day, Hagop!" She said with tears of joy in her eyes.

Hagop rushed eagerly to wake his brother, who was sound asleep.

"Hey, Avo, wake up! It's time for Armenian school."

"Didn't I ask you to call me Abe? I don't like the name Avo. It's a silly Armenian name," he said still half asleep.

"No, yeghpayr (brother), it's a robust, powerful Armenian name. You have to be proud of who you are and where you come from, even if you live in America. Don't follow in my old footsteps. You have to be proud to be American as well as Armenian. I can't wait to tell you about our Badmahayr on the way to school."

"But Jack, I don't want to go to Armenian school," replied Avo.

"Please don't call me Jack. I am Hagop. And yes, little brother, you do. Did you know that we are named Hye after Haig Nahabed? Have you really paid attention to the stories of St. Mesrob Mashdots, St. Gregory the Illuminator, and Sassountzi Tavit? Have you really listened to the stories of Soseh Mayrig, the Fedayees, and of the Armenians who fought back the Turks and defended our country? Have you heard of the countless famous Armenians like William Saroyan (writer), Cher (singer, actress), System of a Down (band and Armenian rights activists), Arshile Gorky (artist), Charles Aznavour (singer), Dr. Raymond Damadian (creator of the MRI), Raffi (children's songwriter), Ross Bagdasarian (the cartoonist of The Chipmunks), Rien Vartan Long (football player) and so many more?" said Hagop with such enthusiasm that his brother was taken aback.

Vartan Mamigonian

Archile
Gorky

Sassountzi Davit

"Geez, Jack, I mean Hagop, relax! No, I haven't really paid attention, but I'm sure you're going to tell me on our way to school."

"Whether you like it or not!" teased Hagop.

"Oh my goodness, achkes looys." (An Armenian saying that literally means the light of my eye, but used sarcastically when someone is about to go into a very long story.)

Dedication

I thank God for blessing me with so many wonderful people in my life. This book is dedicated first and foremost to my two boys, Hagop Joseph and Avo David. I would also like to thank my husband, Kevork, for always encouraging and supporting me throughout this whole adventure. This work would not have been possible without the help of my many friends and family members particularly my parents, Hagop and Araxi Keoseyan, my dear friends Liza Seropian Yessaian, Tamara Gureghian Kazandjian, Sonya Varoujian, Armineh Markarian Manookian, Elizabeth Davtian, Arpi Dabbaghian, Anita Havatian, Shake Sarkisian Markarian, Tina Marie Keoseyan, Selineh Shahbazian, Rozette Keosseyan Sakadjian, Higo Koushakjian Keoseyan, Taleen Keoseyan Tarpinian, Shushan Muradian, Vartuhi Muradian, Aleen Kechichian, Marie Eve Keoseyan, Maria Dikranian, Melineh Merdjanian, Sandra Burgess, Talin Sesetyan, and everyone who believed in me and encouraged me to reach for my dreams. A special thanks to my friends that endlessly supported me throughout this whole experience.

A special thanks to my Armenian teacher, Mrs. Nazik Sesetyan, and to all of the teachers and Sisters at Armenian Sisters Academy who re-ignited the Armenian flame that my parents instilled in me. Heartfelt gratitude to all of my advisors and counselors in the Armenian Youth Federation and HMEM. Your inspiration helped me to nourish my desire to know my roots. Thanks go out to Hourie Marganian (www.hyemedznank.com) for lending her support and giving me permission to use her product in the story.

Made in the USA
Monee, IL
16 November 2021